W9-BRM-605

CROSS-SECTIONS

THE B-2 SPIRIT STEALTH BOMBER

by Ole Steen Hansen
illustrated by Alex Pang
Consultant: Craig Hoyle, Defense Editor, Flight International

Capstone
press
Mankato, Minnesota

First published in the United States in 2006 by Capstone Press
151 Good Counsel Drive, P.O. Box 669, Mankato, Minnesota 56002
http://www.capstonepress.com

Library of Congress Cataloging-in-Publication Data
Hansen, Ole Steen.
   The B-2 Spirit stealth bomber / by Ole Steen Hansen ; illustrated by Alex Pang.
   p. cm.—(Edge books, cross sections)
   Summary: "An in-depth look at the B-2 Spirit Stealth Bomber, with detailed
cross-section diagrams, action photos, and fascinating facts"—Provided by publisher.
   Includes bibliographical references and index.
   ISBN 0-7368-5255-7 (hardcover)
   1. B-2 bomber—Juvenile literature. I. Pang, Alex, ill. II. Title. II. Series.
UG1242.B6H34 2006
623.74'63—dc22   2005009643

Designed and produced by

David West 🧍🧍 Children's Books
7 Princeton Court
55 Felsham Road
Purney
London SW15 1AZ

Designer: Eric T Budge
Editors: Gail Bushnell, Kate Newport

Photo Credits
U.S. Air Force photo, 1; U.S. Air Force photo by Staff Sgt. Cherie A. Thurlby, 4/5;
NASA, 6bl, 6br, 7t; U.S. Air Force photo, 7tr; Northrop Grumman, 11; U.S. Air
Force photo by Staff Sgt. Cherie A. Thurlby, 12; U.S. Air Force photo, 14b, 15m; U.S.
Air Force photo by Master Sgt. Francis Dupuis, 15t, U.S. Air Force photo by Master
Sgt. Michael R. Nixon, 16/17; U.S. Air Force photo, 18b; Northrop Grumman, 19tl;
U.S. Air Force photo, 20b, 23both; U.S. Air Force photo by Senior Master Sgt. Rose
Reynolds, 25; U.S. Air Force photo by Staff Sgt. Scott T. Sturkol, 25inset; U.S. Navy
photo by Intelligence Specialist 1st Class Kenneth Moll, 28bl; U.S. Navy photo,
28/29b; Corbis, 29; U.S. Air Force photo by Sue Baker, 29tl.

1 2 3 4 5 6 10 09 08 07 06 05

TABLE OF CONTENTS

THE STEALTH BOMBER

The B-2 bomber was created to destroy enemy nuclear missile bases without being seen or shot down. It functions as if it is almost invisible. It cannot be seen by radar. The B-2 is very hard to find with the naked eye. The B-2 is a bomber that can truly surprise the enemy.

The B-2 is the most dangerous big bomber the world has ever seen. It is also the most expensive. Each costs over $1 billion to build. Only the U.S. Air Force uses the B-2.

HISTORY

The B-2 is a flying wing. It doesn't have a body or even a tail. The entire aircraft is a wing.

The Horten flying jet fighter was planned during World War II (1939–1945).

FLYING WINGS

In the 1940s, flying wings were first planned to create less drag, or resistance to the air. With less drag, an aircraft can fly faster and carry a bigger load of fuel and weapons. But flying wings are hard to balance. Test aircraft were found to have nearly the same drag as an ordinary aircraft.

The B-35 (*left*) flying wing was made as a long-range bomber. The smaller N-9M (*below*) was first built to test whether the idea would work.

The YB-49 was a test aircraft for a big flying wing bomber. When a YB-49 crashed in 1948, the project was cancelled. It was decided that the aircraft was not safe to fly.

Three U.S. Air Force bombers: (*from top to bottom*) the B-52, the B-1, and the B-2 stealth bomber.

STEALTH

It was discovered that flying wings are difficult to see on radar. Then the B-2 was specially built as a flying wing to make it stealthy, or difficult for the enemy to find. Every single detail has been designed to make the aircraft almost invisible to radar.

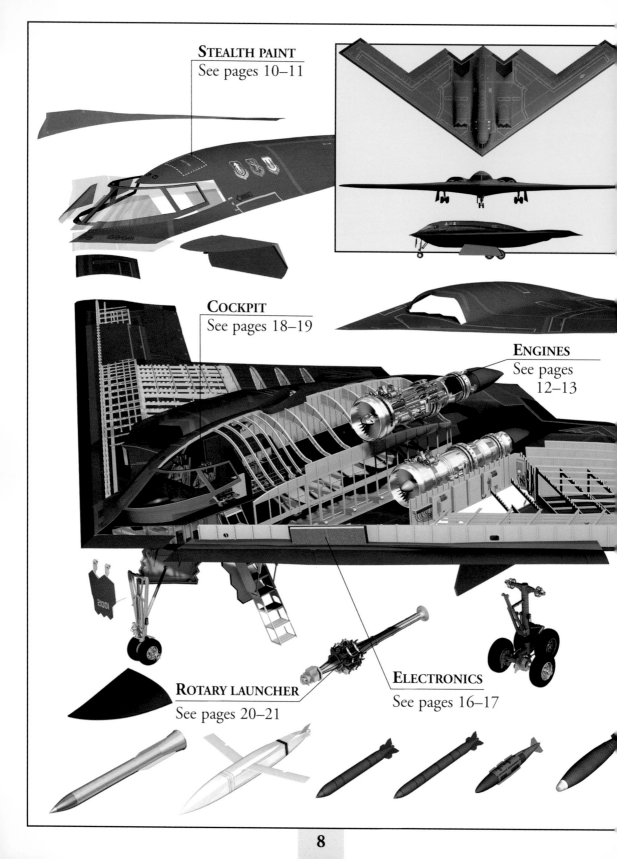

STEALTH PAINT
See pages 10–11

COCKPIT
See pages 18–19

ENGINES
See pages 12–13

ROTARY LAUNCHER
See pages 20–21

ELECTRONICS
See pages 16–17

NORTHROP GRUMMAN
B-2A SPIRIT
Wingspan: 172 feet (52.1 meters)
Length: 69 feet (20.9 meters)
Height: 17 feet (5.1 meters)
Speed: 600 miles
    (980 kilometers) per hour
Takeoff Weight: 336,500
    pounds (152,600 kilograms)

CROSS-SECTION

Take a look inside the B-2 stealth bomber. The labels show which pages will help you find out more.

Building a large stealth aircraft is a tough job. It took many years to design and build the B-2. To find the right materials, more than 900 different metals, plastics, and other materials were tested. In 1997, the B-2 was ready to fly missions with the U.S. Air Force.

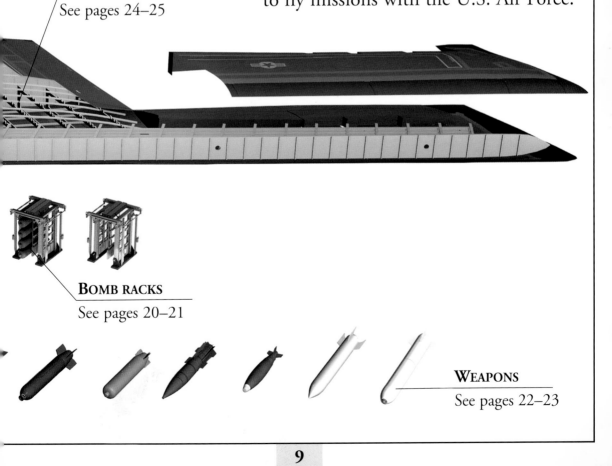

FUEL TANKS
See pages 24–25

BOMB RACKS
See pages 20–21

WEAPONS
See pages 22–23

THE SHAPE

The B-2's shape makes it nearly invisible to radar. But for an aircraft to be stealthy, the hot exhaust needs to be hidden too.

Radar works by sending out invisible beams. When these beams hit parts of an aircraft, they are reflected back to the radar and appear on a screen. But curved shapes send the beams in all different directions. When the beams do not return, the radar operator cannot tell if there is an aircraft in the sky.

STEALTH PAINT

When the Sun's rays hit an aircraft, it warms up. The paint used on the B-2 only slightly heats up. This makes the B-2 hard to find with infrared heat-seeking equipment.

Stealth paint absorbs some of the radar.

Cool exhaust is not picked up by heat-seeking or infrared equipment.

Curved shape scatters radar. None is sent back to enemy receivers.

Enemy radar

NO TAIL FIN
The B-2 has no tail fin because radar would be able to detect its sharp angles.

The B-2's rounded shapes are made from molded composite materials. Metal would be very hard to bend this way. There would be lots of joints between the panels. But composite materials can be made into almost any shape, and there are hardly any joints.

ENGINE EXHAUST

The exhaust flows over the rear wing. As it does so it cools down slightly so that the enemy cannot find it with infrared heat-seeking equipment.

ANTI-RADAR PANELS

All panels and hatches must be made completely smooth on the B-2's surface. Anything sticking out just a little could be spotted by radar.

ANTI-RADAR SHAPE

A combination of straight lines and curves is best at scattering the enemy's radar beams.

AIR INTAKE
Air is sucked in by large fans at the front of the engine.

COMPRESSOR
The compressor blades turn at high speed and compress the air.

COMBUSTION CHAMBER
Fuel is burned here with the compressed air.

BYPASS DUCT
Some of the cold air from the fan passes through the bypass duct.

THE ENGINE

Jet engines create hot gases. Infrared and other heat-seeking equipment can detect the heat from the exhaust.

The B-2's engines are hidden on top of the wing. This makes them more difficult for infrared equipment on the ground to discover. Hot air from the B-2's exhaust is mixed with cold bypass air from a fan. The exhaust cools quickly and keeps the plane hidden.

ENGINES SPECIFICATIONS
The B-2 has four General Electric F118-GE-100 turbofan engines, each rated at 19,000 lbs of thrust. More powerful engines are not needed, because the B-2 has very low drag.

A Boeing 767-300 airliner weighs less than a B-2, but has about 50 percent more engine power. In spite of this, the B-2 flies at the same speed because of low drag.

EXHAUSTS
The hot gases are forced backward, which provides the thrust to push the aircraft forward.

B-2 IN FLIGHT

On the B-2, all control surfaces are built into the trailing edge of the wing.

Most aircraft have a rudder, elevator, and ailerons that control them. The B-2 has all of these controls on the trailing edge of the wing. Like other aircraft, a central computer in the cockpit runs the control surfaces. Control surfaces help the pilot to guide the plane.

A B-2 prepares to land. The aircraft has little drag. To slow it down, the outboard ailerons split open and act as air brakes.

ELEVATOR
The elevator in the middle is used to keep the B-2 steady while it flies in gusty air at low level.

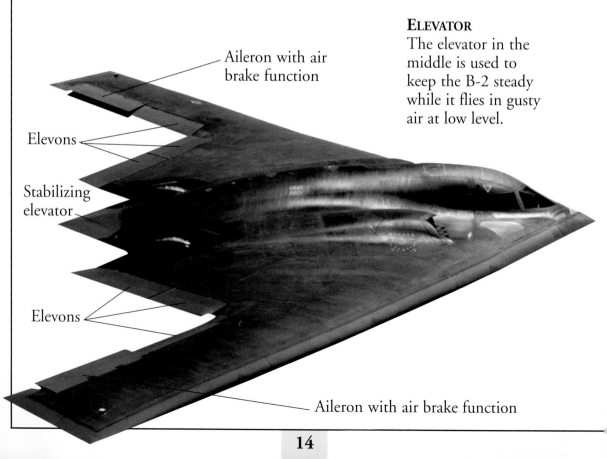

Aileron with air brake function

Elevons

Stabilizing elevator

Elevons

Aileron with air brake function

In moist air and at high speed, a cloud forms around the B-2.

ROLL
To roll the aircraft to the left, the elevons on the left wing move up. The elevons on the right wing move down.

CLIMB OR DIVE
To make the aircraft climb, the control surfaces on both wings move up. To make the B-2 dive, the pilot moves all control surfaces down.

ELECTRONICS

The electronics on the B-2 help the crew know their location, find their bomb targets, and watch enemy defenses.

1

1

The B-2 crew members navigate using a Global Positioning System (GPS). This tool helps the crew know their exact position. But because the aircraft is stealthy, it can sometimes become a problem if no one else knows their position. In peacetime, the B-2 sends out signals so that air traffic controllers can track it and make sure the bomber flies safely among other aircraft.

1. EW ANTENNAS Antennas for electronic warfare (EW) are used to track enemy radar signals.

2. ASTRO NAVIGATION SENSOR

This system uses images of the stars to help the crew navigate. This is one of the many navigation systems on the B-2.

3. FLUSH ANTENNA PANELS

All antennas are made to lie flat against the surface of the B-2. This design helps to keep the B-2 stealthy. Any antenna sticking out would be easy for enemy radar to find.

4. RADAR UNITS

The radar antennas are made from more than 400 parts. The radar is used as little as possible because the enemy may notice the radar signals.

The B-2 flies very long missions. The electronics make it possible to hit a target even in complete darkness.

CREW AND FLIGHT DECK

The B-2 is flown by a two-person crew. If anything happens to one pilot, the other pilot can finish the mission alone.

It is possible for one pilot to fly the B-2. Computers and the auto pilot system help fly the aircraft, find targets, and guide the B-2 back home. The pilots sit in ejection seats that can blast through roof panels. The panels are made to burst open when the seats are fired.

Pilots may have to stay in the B-2 for nearly two days. A mission can last over 40 hours.

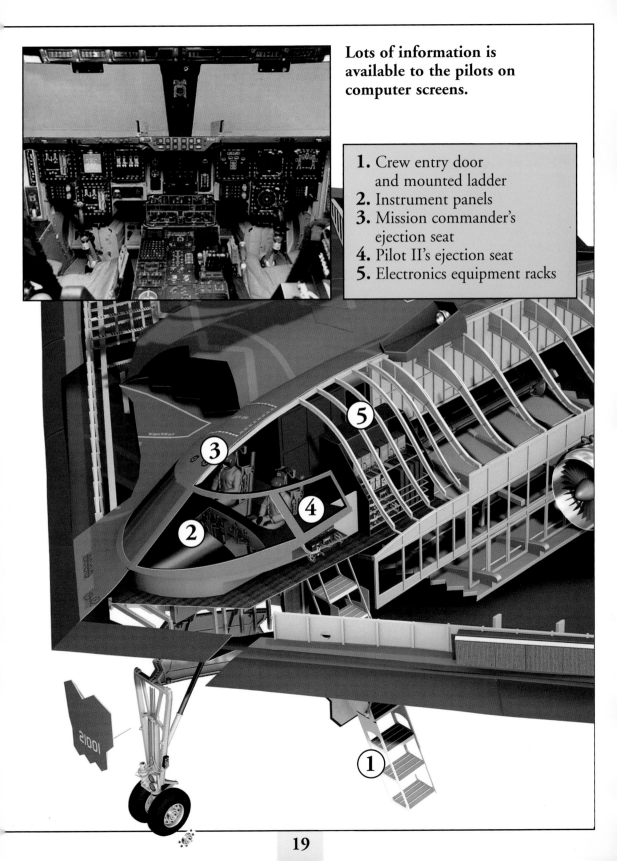

Lots of information is available to the pilots on computer screens.

1. Crew entry door and mounted ladder
2. Instrument panels
3. Mission commander's ejection seat
4. Pilot II's ejection seat
5. Electronics equipment racks

WEAPONS BAYS

On a stealth bomber, the weapons are hidden inside. Any weapons kept under the wings could be seen on radar.

The bombs on the B-2 are stored in two weapons bays. Most bombs are placed on a rotary launcher. The launcher turns and drops the bombs one by one. For the few moments when the weapons bay doors are open, the B-2 will show up on an enemy's radar screen. But by then it is too late for the enemy to stop the B-2's bombs from hitting their target.

THE UNDERSIDE
This view from underneath the B-2 shows the weapons bays.

The B-2 was made to bomb enemy targets. The big stealth bomber can carry up to 40,000 pounds (18,144 kilograms) of bombs.

20

The port (pilot's left) weapons bay has been loaded with bombs.

The starboard (pilot's right) weapons bay has not been loaded yet. The weapons bay rotary launcher can be seen.

BOMB RACK

Smaller bombs are stored on a bomb rack. There are two in each weapons bay.

ROTARY LAUNCHER

The rotary launcher is used for larger weapons, such as nuclear bombs and cruise missiles. There is a launcher in each weapons bay.

WEAPONS

The B-2 was made to destroy Soviet nuclear missile bases. The B-2 would have used nuclear bombs on these missile sites. But attacking these sites never became necessary.

The B-2 can drop almost any kind of bomb, including old-fashioned freefall bombs and cluster bombs that scatter small bombs over a wide area. But the B-2 usually drops "smart" GPS-guided bombs that are sent straight to the targets.

KEY TO DIAGRAM
1. B-83 nuclear weapon
2. B-61 nuclear weapon
3. Mk 82 500-pound bomb
4. Mk 62 mine
5. CBU 87 CEM small weapons dispenser
6. CBU-89 Gator small weapons dispenser
7. Mk 84 2,000 pound bomb
8. GBU-31 2,000 pound Joint Direct Attack Munition (JDAM)
9. GQM-113
10. GAM-84
11. Joint Stand-Off Weapon (JSOW)
12. B61-11 nuclear weapon

The B-2 can drop up to 80 freefall 500-pound (227-kilogram) bombs. But it is more likely that the B-2 will drop one or two "smart" bombs at a time (*below*).

AIR-TO-AIR REFUELING

B-2s have flown the longest combat missions in history. This is possible because B-2s can refuel while in flight.

On a very long mission, a B-2 may have to meet a tanker aircraft several times. On the right, a KC-135 delivers fuel to a B-2.

Air-to-air refueling requires very careful flying. The bomber and the tanker must fly very close to each other, even in bad weather or at night, without crashing. First the B-2 pilot flies the aircraft into position behind and below the tanker. Then a boom operator in the tanker lowers the boom into the B-2's refueling tank.

KEY TO DIAGRAM
1. Starboard outer fuel tanks
2. Starboard rear tank
3. Starboard inboard fuel tanks
4. Port outer fuel tanks
5. Port rear fuel tanks
6. Port inboard fuel tanks
7. Inflight refueling receptacle

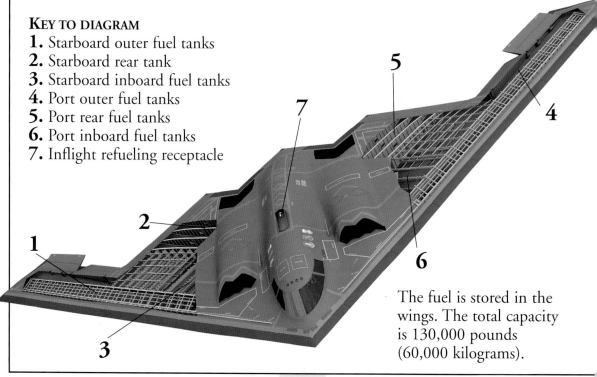

The fuel is stored in the wings. The total capacity is 130,000 pounds (60,000 kilograms).

THE MISSION

As we have seen, the B-2 is a stealth bomber that can fly long distances to hit a target anywhere in the world.

The best thing about the B-2 is that it does not need fighters to protect it. Here is a typical mission to show how the stealth bomber can sneak up on the enemy without them ever knowing that it is there.

5. The B-2 lands at Whiteman airbase after having been airborne for 35 hours.

1. A B-2 takes off from the Whiteman airbase in Missouri. It climbs to 40,000 feet (12,200 meters).

4. The B-2 is low on fuel, so it links up with a tanker. Two refuelings may be needed on a flight across the Atlantic Ocean.

3. The bomb hits the building 45 seconds later. The B-2 is already on its invisible way back to base.

2. The B-2 approaches the target unseen by radar or infrared. An enemy headquarters building is the target. A smart bomb is fired 6 miles (10 kilometers) away from the target.

THE FUTURE

The B-2 is the best long-distance bomber the world has ever seen. But is it still necessary?

The B-2 might be the world's last big bomber, but because it is a stealth bomber, it gives the crew the best chance of finishing a mission without any trouble.

Many targets can be destroyed more cheaply by other weapons. But it is impossible to predict what enemies the United States will have to face in the future. The B-2 is the only bomber that can hide from the enemy so well that it can't be shot down.

Cruise missiles fired from ships are a cheaper way to hit targets. The B-2 can fire them too, but it is an expensive aircraft for the job.

Unmanned aircraft, like this Global Hawk, are being built to locate long-distance targets without risking the lives of pilots.

Raytheon

GLOSSARY

composite materials (kahm-PAH-zit muh-TIH-ree-uhlz)—a special mixture of materials for superior performance

contrails (KON-trayls)—white lines that can be seen from the ground after they are left in the sky behind an aircraft

infrared (in-fruh-RED)—equipment that detects objects by the heat they give off

navigate (NAV-uh-gate)—to travel in an aircraft using instruments to help guide the aircraft

radar (RAY-dar)—equipment that uses radio waves to find or guide objects

refueling (ree-FYOO-ling)—to take on extra fuel so that an aircraft can remain in the air longer

stealth (STELTH)—the ability to fly without being detected by radar

thrust (THRUHST)—the force that pushes an aircraft forward

unmanned (un-MAND)—able to fly by remote control instead of with a crew

READ MORE

Basmadjian, E. E. *The B-2 Spirit.* U.S. Warplanes. New York: Rosen Central, 2003.

Berliner, Don. *Stealth Fighters and Bombers.* Aircraft. Berkeley Heights, N.J.: Enslow, 2001.

Holden, Henry M. *Air Force Aircraft.* Aircraft. Berkeley Heights, N.J.: Enslow, 2001.

Sweetman, Bill. *Stealth Bombers: The B-2 Spirits.* War Planes. Mankato, Minn.: Capstone Press, 2001.

INTERNET SITES

FactHound offers a safe, fun way to find Internet sites related to this book. All of the sites on FactHound have been researched by our staff.

Here's how:
1. Visit *www.facthound.com*
2. Type in this special code **736852557** for age-appropriate sites. Or enter a search word related to this book for a more general search.
3. Click on the **Fetch It** button.

FactHound will fetch the best sites for you!

INDEX